FREDERIK IX AND QUEEN INGRID
The Modern Royal Couple

by Jens Gunni Busck

CW00553665

Historika

Published in cooperation with the Royal Danish Collection

The so-called "Four Kings Picture" in which the first four heads of state from the House of Glücksburg are gathered. Christian IX holds his great-grandchild Prince Frederik (IX), and is flanked by his son and heir Crown Prince Frederik (VIII) and his son Prince Christian (X). A famous photo at the time, taken at Prince Frederik's christening in 1899.

CONTENTS

FOREWORD

Frederik IX and Queen Ingrid were the parents of Her Majesty Queen Margrethe II and her two younger sisters. The popular couple modernized the Royal House with their "informal formality" and became a symbol of an exemplary nuclear family.

This little book tells of matters including Frederik IX's sailing life and love of music, the dramatic years of the German occupation, and Queen Ingrid's varied work within the family and in public.

Birgit Jenvold
Museum Curator

A photogenic Crown Couple travelling by train in 1939.

Frederik IX and Queen Ingrid with their daughters in Greenlandic national dress in 1953. The Royal Couple had just visited Greenland and on that occasion been presented with the outfits. Queen Ingrid invited the press to a photo session followed by Greenlandic "kaffemik", a social gathering centred on drinking coffee, at Gråsten Palace. The pictures circulated around the world's press as it was highly unusual for royalty to wear "ethnic" dress from a colony. Greenland, like the Faroe Islands, is an old Danish possession in the North Atlantic. The Faroe Islands were granted home rule in 1948; Greenland, which was granted home rule in 1979 after having been a Danish county since 1953, has had autonomy since 2009 and is still linked to Denmark. The Royal Family still often visits both the Faroe Islands and Greenland, and happily wears the local national dress.

THE COUPLE WHO REINVENTED THE MONARCHY

In 1955 Frederik IX accompanied his eldest daughter, Princess Margrethe, to Copenhagen Central Station, as she was to attend a boarding school in England. A father can hardly avoid feeling a little worried when his fifteen-year-old daughter leaves home, and according to the Queen's account this was expressed in a very strange way. In parting her father took her by the shoulders and said, half singing in German, "Leb' wohl, du kühnes, herrliches Kind!" (Farewell, you bold, wonderful child!) The King's words were Wotan's parting words to his daughter Brünnhilde in Wagner's opera Die Walküre.

Very few, it must be presumed, quote Wagner operas when saying goodbye to their children, but the episode says much about the preceding Danish monarch. It is evidence of the King's warm-hearted playfulness and of the mode of address in the cultivated home at Amalienborg. And it also attests to Frederik IX's great passion for music. For a true music lover, musical references are an integral part of one's emotional life, and the opera quotation should perhaps be understood as directly expressing that the King was moved rather than as a humorous attempt to hide this fact.

Frederik IX was the most well-liked king Denmark has yet had. This was in part due to the age in which he reigned, for the broad popular enthusiasm for the Royal Family could only really assert itself once the monarchy had relinquished political power. But is was also due to the fact that Frederik IX had a personality which enabled him to take on the role of King of Denmark in the postwar era in an exemplary way. Apart from it being satisfying for the Danish populace to have

The Royal Family's most important refuge, the hunting lodge in Trend by the Limfjord. Frederik IX's Bentley with the number plate 461 is parked in front of the house, the number being the one he was enrolled in the royal yacht Dannebrog's crew inventory with in 1912. The car featured British-style right-hand drive as in Britain, which the King found more desirable.

a tall and handsome king who could both sail a ship and conduct a symphony orchestra with great skill, Frederik IX also mastered the difficult balancing act of being at eye level with the populace and at the same time maintaining the particular grandeur which befits a monarch.

Frederik IX's popularity as king wasn't all his own doing. When he finally got married as a thirty-five-year-old Crown Prince it was a cause of great jubilation, but no one at the time could predict the extent to which the then-Princess Ingrid of Sweden would come to safeguard the future of the Royal Family in Denmark. Apart from the fact that she helped her husband to fulfil his office, her children and grandchildren also learned from her how to bear royal dignity in a harmonious way. Frederik IX and Queen Ingrid were the Royal Couple who completed the Royal Family's gradual disconnection from political power, which had been underway since the introduction of the Constitution in 1849. With the birth of one of them in 1899 and the death of the other in 2000, their time spanned the entirety of the previous century, and as the Royal Couple they made a significant mark on Danish history.

Prince Frederik's Childhood

On 26 May 1898 the royal yacht Dannebrog docked in Copenhagen with the new-lyweds Prince Christian (X) and Princess Alexandrine on board. They had cele-brated their wedding in Cannes a month previously. The couple began their life in common at Sorgenfri Palace, where they quickly met the expectations con-cerning a future heir, as Princess Alexandrine gave birth to a healthy son on 11 March 1899. The christening was held on 9 April, and the son was given the name Christian Frederik Franz Michael Carl Valdemar Georg, shortened in fam-ily circles to Rico. The following year the family moved into the newly renovat-

The princes with Chris-tian X in the unusu-al role of donkey driver at Sorgenfri Palace in 1905. Prince Frederik and Prince Knud were very fond of Polly the donkey, which Prince Knud was given by their grandmother, Grand Duchess Anastasia, on his fourth birthday. For unknown reasons the donkey was called "the Tailor" by the stable personnel.

The princes were
for a time partici-
pants in the Danish
scouting movement,
which has existed
since 1909. Prince
Frederik, however,
showed very little
interest in scouting.

ed Christian VIII's Palace at Amalienborg, and in July 1900 Rico got a younger brother, Prince Knud. The first years were quiet and fairly idyllic, but the boys' childhood wouldn't be entirely easy. Despite his sensitive nature Prince Christian was far from loving towards his sons, and his work as captain of the Life Guards rubbed off on the home, where a certain atmosphere of the barracks was felt. The little princes lived under an ever present threat of corporeal punishment, although Princess Alexandrine's mild nature was a comforting element.

In their childhood Prince Frederik and Prince Knud spent much time outdoors and there are many accounts of them according to which they were not entirely easy to control. It is probable that their unruliness had to do with boredom, since they seldom saw other playmates than one another. The brothers received a strict and thorough schooling at Amalienborg Primary School (later Middle School), which was established for their sake and only had two pupils. The two princes were therefore very close as children, though they grew apart later in life.

Christian IX died in 1906, after which Frederik VIII became King and Prince Christian became Crown Prince. This made the family more interesting to the public, but the princes continued their upbringing in calm surroundings, since the media coverage of the boys was very modest in comparison with coverage of royalty in our own time.

The Musical Teenager

The first great change in Prince Frederik's life occurred in May 1912 when Frederik VIII died in Hamburg on his way home from a health cure. His parents thus became the new Royal Couple, and the thirteen-year-old Frederik now became Crown Prince and a Knight of the Order of the Elephant. The change of monarch meant that there was much more focus on the family, which in particular the Crown Prince and the Queen had difficulty getting used to. His schooling naturally continued as usual, but around this time Crown Prince Frederik was also gripped by his passion for music, which would shape him throughout his life.

Alexandrine had noticed early on that her eldest son listened attentively when she played the piano, which she mastered to a high amateur level. She had tak-

Frederik IX and Queen Ingrid

en Prince Frederik with her to the opera as early as 1909, even though her husband thought it a peculiar idea, and the ten-year-old was enthusiastic. In the summer of 1911 he began to take piano lessons with a young teacher called Lizzy Hohlenberg, with whom he remained in contact for the rest of his life. An experience of decisive importance for the young Crown Prince was a performance of Peer Gynt in 1913, to which Queen Alexandrine had brought the score; the experience of seeing the printed notes on the page and hearing Edvard Grieg's orchestral music was apparently seminal for him. Following this he took lessons in conducting, music theory, and the reading of scores with the conductor of the same performance, Georg Høeberg, in whose home the Crown Prince became a frequent guest.

Crown Prince Frederik's circle of friends gradually came to encompass several talented musicians, and between 1916 and 1919 a circle of musicians gathered each Saturday at Amalienborg with the Crown Prince conducting, typically with Queen Alexandrine at the piano.

Amalienborg Middle School became Amalienborg Højere Almenskole (equivalent to the later years of Secondary or Grammar School) and the Crown Prince took his 'studentereksamen' (equivalent to A-levels) in 1917. A few months earlier he had celebrated his eighteenth birthday, an occasion that had attracted much attention. Heirs to the throne came of age at eighteen, and Frederik was now granted him a seat in the Privy Council. At a specially arranged meeting of the Privy Council, Christian X held a moving speech for his son, in which he instructed him to have the courage of his convictions. The Home Secretary, Ove Rode of the Danish Social Liberal Party, described the event in his diary with a remark that the Crown Prince would in his future office have to decide to have no convictions and be uncompromising in that conviction. Such an attitude actually became very characteristic of Frederik IX as king, but more of that later.

The Crown Prince at Sea

As a child Crown Prince Frederik had loved to be on board the royal yacht Dannebrog in the summer, and even as a ten-year-old he had declared that he wanted to be a sailor. In order to avoid too much mischief on board, he and Prince Knud

The King conducted the Royal Orchestra on recordings for the benefit of UN aid in 1948.

In the weeks leading up to the Reunification with Southern Jutland in 1920, Crown Prince Frederik and Prince Knud had to practice horse riding so that they could accompany Christian X on his ride across the border. During the border ride the Crown Prince's horse began to walk sideways once they had passed the triumphal arch, which was the source of much amusement amongst his fellow officers in the navy. According to Queen Anne-Marie, Frederik IX later formulated his opinion of the four-legged creatures thus: "Horses are dangerous at the front, dangerous at the back, and uncomfortable in the middle."

had been included in the ship's register, i.e. the crew numbers which are used to share out chores, after which the princes were given a number of practical chores on the ship. Crown Prince Frederik was given the number 461 and felt so attached to it that he later used it as the number plate on his cars.

That the Crown Prince chose to train as a naval officer was, however, a stark break in tradition, for every Danish king since Christian IV had had a close relationship with the army. Christian X in no way condoned his son's career choice and tried to convince him to become an army officer, but to no avail. The Crown Prince wanted to go to sea, and this was presumably his greatest rebellion against his stubborn father, who apparently never forgave him. This is perhaps one of the reasons why Crown Prince Frederik never became a member of the freemasons, of which organization Christian X and Frederik VIII before him had been Grand Masters.

In the summer of 1917 the Crown Prince went on the obligatory apprentice voyage with the cruiser Heimdal, and thereafter began attending the Cadet School. In accordance with his own and his parents' wishes he was treated the same as his mates, although he didn't live at the school during the training. It soon became clear that the particular culture of the navy suited the Crown Prince wonderfully.

Whereas the army was the place for draconian discipline and strict hierarchies, social conventions in the navy were more relaxed and friendly. Rank and rules of course apply on a ship too, but because officers and recruits are literally in the same boat and subject to the vagaries of the sea, the sense of affinity is greater. A few years later Prince Knud also attended the navy's cadet school, though the brothers didn't see much of each other in that context.

Crown Prince Frederik took his naval officer's examination in September 1921, but continued his education in the following years, as he was gradually given more responsibilities. In the 1920s he served on inspection ships, coastal defence

Lieutenant Commander Crown Prince Frederik on board the torpedo ship Hvalrossen (the Walrus), of which he was the commander in 1933 and again in 1934. The close comradeship at sea, of which the officers are also a part, made a decisive impression on the Crown Prince, and his career in the navy was of defining importance for his later reign. His time at sea taught him to behave with a natural authority which at the same time seemed unpretentious and straightforward.

Hunting was one of
the traditional royal
amusements which
Crown Prince Fred-
erik enjoyed. Here
he is seen at the be-
ginning of the 1930s
with Prince Axel (on
the right) and an
unknown hunting
friend.

ships, and in particular torpedo ships. In 1927 the Crown Prince was given command of his own ship, as he was for a time the commander of the torpedo ship Søhunden, and further, corresponding assignments came in the following years. In 1929 he was named Lieutenant Commander and in 1935 Commander. The only naval ships he didn't sail with were the submarines, which didn't interest him.

A Bachelor in Uniform

As an eighteen-year-old Crown Prince Frederik was given an apartment in an annexe to Christian VIII's Palace at Amalienborg, facing Frederiksgade, where he lived throughout his years as a bachelor. As his career in the navy progressed, he was given yet more royal commitments and accompanied his parents to most official events. One of his new passions was cars, and he liked to drive fast in his new models. Music also continued to play a major part in his life. The Crown Prince built up an impressive record collection and almost always followed the score while he listened. He often had the opportunity to conduct the Life Guards and the Navy's Music Corps, and loved to go to concerts and the theatre.

The Crown Prince also began hunting and rowing at quite a young age, and these later became important forms of recreation for him. He also traveled often and in 1930 went, for example, on a lengthy voyage to East Asia with Prince Knud and their uncle Prince Axel and his wife Princess Margaretha.

In general, however, Crown Prince Frederik spent as much of his youth as possible in the company of his mates in the navy, of which several became friends for life. It was in the navy, far from his father's old-fashioned court, that he met people from other social classes, and the straightforward and informal modes of address suited his friendly, down-to-earth nature. It was also in the navy, however, that he got used to a carefree drinking culture, which laid the foundations of his later overconsumption of alcohol. The Crown Prince's life in the 1920s and early 1930s was of course also characterized by a degree of partying and relationships with women. He looked unusually good in his officer's uniform, and the girls swooned over him wherever he went.

In 1922 Crown Prince Frederik was briefly engaged to Princess Olga of Greece. They were both great-grandchildren of Christian IX and had met one another in

Cannes, but the Princess ended their engagement just two months later. This was officially explained as a disinclination to convert to the Evangelical Lutheran Church, but in private correspondence it was clear that she couldn't come to terms with Crown Prince Frederik's 'sailor's habits'. This wasn't something he took badly, but many years were to pass before the Crown Prince got engaged again.

Princess Ingrid's Road to Denmark

Crown Prince Frederik and Princess Ingrid met for the first time at the summer palace Sofiero by the Øresund in the summer of 1917, when she was a girl of seven and he had just finished school. At that time they would probably both have been rather surprised if one had presented them with the possibility of a future marriage.

Denmark's most eligible bachelor in 1929.

Princess Ingrid with her mother, Crown Princess Margaret of Sweden, and her two elder brothers. Her mother's death a few years later was the overshadowing event in the Princess's upbringing and marked her for the rest of her life.

Ingrid Victoria Sofia Louise Margareta was born on 28 March 1910 as the only daughter of Crown Prince Gustaf (later VI) Adolf of Sweden and Crown Princess Margaret, who was the grandchild of Queen Victoria of the United Kingdom. Princess Ingrid grew up with two elder and two younger brothers and was given an upbringing that was very modern for the time. Creative subjects had an important place in her schooling and interested the Princess much more than academic ones. Due to hereditary dyslexia she was slow in learning to read, and she declared at a young age that she wanted to be an actress. One of her brothers has since stated, however, that his sister had understood at a very young age that she would marry and leave the country.

In Crown Princess Margaret, Princess Ingrid had a complete role model, who apart from being a loving and caring mother was also creative, beautiful, disciplined (she didn't, for example, eat meat or drink alcohol) and extremely popular with the Swedish people. It was therefore a genuine catastrophe for the ten-year-old Princess Ingrid when her mother unexpectedly died during a pregnancy in 1920 as the result of complications during a trivial case of otitis. This was the end of a happy childhood, for after this Princess Ingrid began to live according to her mother's ideals and took on, as the only woman in the family, the role of a grown woman. She became dutiful, hardworking, and persistent, and fought a daily battle to achieve the exorbitant goals she set herself. Her father remarried in 1923, but Princess Ingrid's relationship with her stepmother never became warm.

Ingrid developed into the very model of a modern, active woman, who could both play tennis, ride a horse, ski, and skate. She cut her hair short, passed her driving test, and went on a diet so she could fit the fashionable clothing she showed an advanced taste in early on.

As early as 1928 rumours arose for the first time about a relationship between Princess Ingrid and the Danish Crown Prince, because he had accompanied her to a ballet in Stockholm. The press saw an obvious marriage alliance, as both were of marriageable age and highly sought-after matches, who furthermore knew each other well due to the close ties between the Danish and Swedish Royal Families. In the papers Princess Ingrid was also for a while connected with the Prince of Wales, but nothing happened on either front until 1933, when the Crown Prince was in Stockholm to see Wagner's Ring Cycle – which he was

later to quote to his daughter in Copenhagen Central Station. Several members of the Swedish Royal Family, including Princess Ingrid, went with him, and in the ensuing time the Crown Prince undertook many visits to Sweden. This led to ever more persistent rumours in the press, but it wasn't made publicly known that the Danish Crown Prince had a proposal rejected at the beginning of 1934. Despithe this rejection, however, they kept in contact, even while Princess Ingrid was on a long journey to Asia later in the year.

At the end of January 1935 the Crown Prince was to go to Stockholm in the company of his musical mentor Georg Høeberg, who was to conduct there. A few days before departure, however, Crown Prince Frederik almost choked on his morning coffee when he read in the newspaper Berlingske Tidende that his engagement to Ingrid was to be declared during the coming visit. It was a large blot in the royalist newspaper's copy when Christian X released a sharply worded denial via the Private Secretary's Office, and Crown Prince Frederik even considered cancelling the trip. But on 2 February he travelled all the same, and two days later he returned home with Princess Ingrid's commitment to marriage.

The Marriage and the First Years

On 14 March 1935 Queen Alexandrine and Crown Prince Frederik went to Stockholm, where an army of journalists was waiting at the train station. They waited in vain, for Princess Ingrid had fetched the guests in her car at Södertälje, approximately 25 km outside Stockholm. The press got what they were after though, as the engagement was announced the same evening. The following day the joy at the coming marriage was silenced for a while, as Queen Alexandrine was diagnosed with volvulus, but she pulled through after a few critical days.

Princess Ingrid's first official visit to Denmark on 11 April caused overwhelming jubilation, and the wedding itself was to be held in Stockholm as early as May. Crown Prince Frederik is said to have preferred a modest family wedding, but instead he got a grandiose marathon celebration which lasted for six days. The ceremony took place in Stockholm Cathedral on 24 May, while the Swedish capital was in the grips of a wedding ecstasy. Later the same day the new-

Christian X kisses his newlywed daughter-in-law on her arrival in Copenhagen on 26 May 1935 after the sailing trip home on the Dannebrog. Crown Princess Ingrid was one of the few who could soften Christian X up. The date also had a special meaning for the family and was hardly randomly chosen: on 26 May 1842 Prince Christian (IX) and Princess Louise, who had founded the House of Glücksburg, got married at Amalienborg, where they also celebrated a grand golden wedding anniversary on 26 May 1892. And on 26 May 1898 Prince Christian X and Princess Alexandrine arrived in Copenhagen aboard Dannebrog after having held their wedding in Cannes a month earlier.

The Crown Couple's
journey to the USA
in 1939 took them
to California; the
photograph shows
them by a giant red-
wood there. The car
is decorated with
an Icelandic flag as
well as the Danish
and American ones.
This is due to the
fact that Iceland
was at the time in a
so-called personal
union with Denmark,
as the country had
since 1917 had po-
litical autonomy.
Iceland gained in-
dependence from
the Danish Crown in
1944.

lyweds boarded the royal yacht Dannebrog, which sailed them to Copenhagen, a trip they had arranged by letting Princess Ingrid ask Christian X for permission to borrow the royal yacht for the occasion. The King was from the beginning exceedingly enthusiastic about his new daughter-in-law, and Crown Prince Frederik would probably never himself have gained such permission from his father. On 26 May the newlywed Crown Couple were granted a reception at which all the ceremonial pomp was rolled out. The authorities estimated that half a million Copenhageners had lined the streets along the carriage's route later in the day. The following day ended, furthermore, with a gala performance in the Royal Theatre at which Georg Høeberg conducted the first act of Die Valkyrie, which was on the programme in honour of the opera-loving bridegroom.

The Crown Couple honeymooned in Rome, which thereafter became their favoured holiday destination. They continued to Paris and Brussels, and immediately on returning went on an exhaustive tour of Denmark, during which they were celebrated across the entire country.

It quickly became clear that it was two quite different people who had married. While the Crown Prince was outgoing, emotional, and by royal standards quite coarse in his language, his wife was in contrast buttoned up. She was extremely self-controlled, and many Danes found her to be too rigid and correct, although it was of course not something the press delved into as they would have today. Crown Princess Ingrid made the effort, however, to learn fluent Danish very quickly, and in the course of a few years became far more smiling and extrovert. Presumably her straightforward husband had a positive influence in this respect, and there was no doubt a reciprocal good influence. In spite of his extrovert nature, Crown Prince Frederik could still feel nervous about his future reign, and Princess Ingrid took it upon herself to help her husband overcome his insecurity and grow into taking on his responsibilities. Life together required a couple of years of reciprocal adaption, but thereafter the Royal Couple became allied to an unusual degree. When they were together, the Crown Prince wasn't too familiar and matey, and the Crown Princess wasn't too distant and reserved, so they complemented each other wonderfully.

Their initial time together was marked by the comprehensive restoration of Frederik VIII's Palace at Amalienborg, which Crown Princess Ingrid led expertly. She involved herself in all the details, was given all the plans to look over,

and wandered each day across the palace square to inspect the work, as the Crown Couple were temporarily accommodated in the palace opposite. Crown Prince Frederik managed to force through, however, that his own office be given the same colours and furnishings as the digs of his youth. A month after moving in the Crown Couple were also able to begin using Gråsten Palace near Flensburg Firth as a summer residence, which was a cause of joy in Southern Jutland, and with the people's gift of 430,000 DKK which they had received on their marriage they built a hunting lodge on 400 acres of land in Trend Forest near the Limfjord.

The first years of marriage were characterized by frequent travels, for they took on all the state functions they could, both at home and abroad. For example, the Crown Couple sailed to Iceland in 1938 in the company of Queen Alexandrine, and in 1939 they spent two months travelling around the USA, which was their hitherto most important state function and was a resounding success. The beautiful couple attracted overwhelming interest from the American media, and they demonstrated to the utmost that they would be able to tackle their coming office as king and queen.

The War and the Sunshine Princess

Crown Prince Frederik was one of the first to understand that something was up on 9 April 1940. He couldn't sleep and from his bathroom window saw Prime Minister Thorvald Stauning rushing to Christian VIII's Palace at five in the morning. At a meeting with the King which was immediately called, with the participation of the Crown Prince, it was decided that all resistance should be stopped. The 40,000 German troops were more than the 3000 mobilized Danish troops could cope with, and the threat of a bombardment of Copenhagen left no real choice. While the meeting was taking place the Royal Life Guards defended Amalienborg, and three Guards were injured before Christian X's order to put down arms reached the streets.

"Now it's a matter of holding our heads high and keeping our backs straight," was the heavily pregnant Crown Princess Ingrid's assessment of the situation. Due to the unusually warm relations she enjoyed with her father-in-law, her encouragement was instrumental in moving the King to continue his daily rides through the streets of Copenhagen the very next day. This was of great importance for the populace as a symbolic expression of the country's resilience.

The Royal Family were kept under surveillance, but were free to move about and tried to live as normal a life as possible. For the Crown Couple, however, everything wasn't as normal, for exactly a week after the invasion, on 16 April, the Crown Princess bore a healthy daughter weighing 3300 grams. The birth

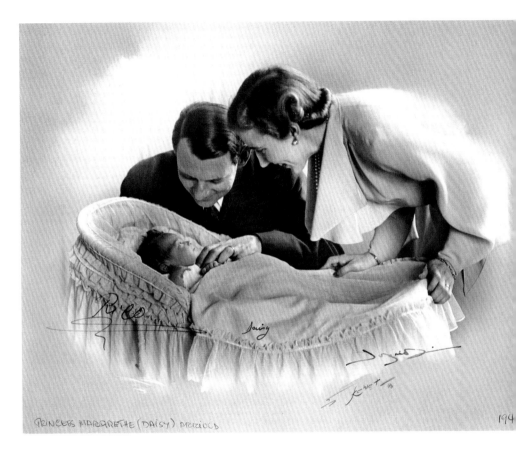

PRINCESS MARGRETHE (DAISY) PERIOD   194

was a twenty-four hour ordeal, but Princess Margrethe's arrival was on the other hand a welcome event for the Danes. In a dark time good news was needed, and the Royal Family was something people could rally around as a kind of open space for the cowed national sentiment. Immediately on being born little Princess Margrethe became a national icon, and to the pleasure of her parents her characteristic "princess quiff" started a fashion.

Fatherhood and the occupation greatly curbed Crown Prince Frederik's activities in the navy, but after having been named a Commander in 1939 he had with customary irony remarked that he was "too important" to sail a ship. The Crown

The birth of Princess Margrethe a week after the Occupation was a ray of light in a dark time. The picture of the cot with the proud parents became a popular motif.

28   Frederik IX and Queen Ingrid

Prince concentrated instead on his family and his state functions, just as he took part in the ongoing meetings between the occupying power, the government, and the King.

In the autumn of 1942 the family's everyday life was turned on its head when the Crown Prince suddenly had to step in as the head of state. In September the so-called Telegram Crisis had arisen when King Christian had on his birthday sent a very brief thank you in reply to Hitler's message of congratulation.

This "insult" was used as an excuse to demand that a more Germanophile government be installed, but before this had been cleared up Christian X was invalided in a riding accident which nearly cost him his life. For the next seven months Crown Prince Frederik had to govern on behalf of the King, and it was also he who had, at the request of Germany, to accept Foreign Minister Erik Scavenius as the new Prime Minister instead of Vilhelm Buhl, who had taken over after Thorvald Stauning's death. Luckily the Crown Prince avoided having to go to Berlin to smooth over the telegram problem, as had been the plan, and thus he also avoided having his appendix removed. He had made an agreement with Rigshospitalet (the national hospital) about staging a false appendicitis in order to avoid an audience with Hitler.

Whilst Crown Prince Frederik officially supported the policy of collaboration, unofficially he adopted a double role and was positive about the growing resistance movement. He kept himself thoroughly oriented about the activities, amongst other things through his contacts in the navy, since his position didn't allow him to involve himself directly. It is certain, however, that weapons and other equipment were kept in the Crown Couple's hunting lodge near the Limfjord, and in all likelihood on the royal yacht Dannebrog.

In May 1943 the King once more took over the responsibility of governing, but as early as 29 August he was in his own words "suspended" when Germany deposed the government and took over its powers. On this occasion no shots were fired at Amalienborg, but things were much more violent when German soldiers arrested more than 2000 policemen and border guards on 19 September 1944, which caused the police who were guarding Amalienborg to hit back forcefully. The fighting, which both the Royal Couple and the Crown Couple could follow from their respective palaces, resulted in twenty dead German soldiers and many wounded.

Die-cut image from the time of the Occupation, which shows the Crown Prince engaged in one of his most important pastimes of that period. Crown Prince Frederik took an interest in rowing at the end of the 1930s, and during the Occupation he rowed out from the Svanemøllen harbour almost every morning during the summer months. He also tried tennis during the same period, but didn't have the same flair for the game as his wife.

The King had his set routines on board the Dannebrog. At 7.45 am he would be woken and went down onto the quarterdeck where an officer stood at the ready with a fire hose. This freezing cold hosing down was carried out in all kinds of weather, even in the Greenlandic cold.

At Amalienborg the Liberation on 5 May 1945 was also dramatic, as the German cruiser Nürnberg refused to surrender and shot at Frederik VIII's Palace just as the Crown Prince and family had sat down to dinner. No one came to any harm, however, and even though Amalienborg was damaged this didn't dampen the joy about the German capitulation.

Expansion of the Family and the Accession

A year before the Liberation, on 29 April 1944, the Crown Couple had become parents for the second time, when Princess Benedikte was born. This was an especially great joy as Crown Princess Ingrid had a year or two previously had a miscarriage and was very troubled by her pregnancies. The Princess's birth wasn't marked by a salute from the Sixtus Battery on the island of Holmen, but by the Resistance, who to the irritation of the occupying power saluted from H.C. Ørsted Park.

The cannons on Holmen came into use two years later, however, when Princess Anne-Marie was born on 30 August 1946. At first the joy at this event was perhaps mixed with disappointment, as ruling royal families were at that time under a certain amount of pressure to produce male heirs. The Crown Couple now had all the children they wanted to have, and as they were all daughters one had to accept that the order of succession would pass to Prince Knud and his son Prince Ingolf. If Crown Prince Frederik was disappointed, his daughters didn't feel it, for he was very proud of his children and just as enamoured of his wife.

The time between the Liberation and the accession was characterized by a number of official functions. Christian X was extremely weakened by his riding accident some years before, and in 1945 had suffered his first heart attack which, however, only kept him in bed for a few days. But at the end of March 1947 the King suffered another heart attack, and after having been further weakened by pneumonia Christian X died surrounded by his family on 20 April 1947.

Frederik IX was in principle king from the moment of his father's death, but the official proclamation took place the following day from the balcony of Chris-

Frederik IX liked to refer to Queen Ingrid and their daughters as his "four-leaf clover". Here the four-leaf clover is seen around the time of the accession.

tiansborg Palace in front of a gathering of 200,000 Danes. After the proclamation itself, the new king stepped forward and made a short but tasteful speech which contained the modest motto With God for Denmark. After he had conducted a ninefold hurrah for Denmark, Queen Ingrid joined him on the balcony, and Frederik IX announced that "we two will now continue according to the example set by our old royal couple!" But when he immediately afterwards gave the Queen a big kiss on the cheek it was clear that new times had been heralded for the Royal Family. Christian X would never have dreamed of doing such a thing, however sensitive he may have been behind the tough facade.

It must be said that Frederik IX was well-prepared for his new office. He was thoroughly schooled in constitutional law and had gained a great deal of practical experience of governance from Christian X's many journeys and from the time of the Occupation. Furthermore, he kept himself well-informed about current affairs at home and abroad, and had an enormous knowledge of all kinds of subjects, which continued to impress the many important people whom the King met during his reign.

From the beginning it was also clear that Denmark had a Queen who would make herself more of a visible presence than Queen Alexandrine had. Queen Ingrid took the leading role in the home while the daughters were growing up, but at the same time took on a wealth of functions, and was granted her own flag and Life Guard Regiment. Queen Ingrid's feminine charm gave her a personal forcefulness which she very much knew how to make use of, just

The Royal Couple are received at Maniitsoq in the late summer of 1952. Frederik IX had sailed to Greenland with the Dannebrog in order to pay the first royal visit there in 31 years. Queen Ingrid chose to fly both ways, as she found the voyage too long. The seas were apparently also so high that even the "sailor king" was seasick, but the trip was a great pleasure for him.

Kong Frederik og Dronning Ingrid fotograferet paa Amalienborg sammen med Prinsesserne Margrethe og Anne-Marie (til venstre) og Benedikte, der sidder paa Kongens Skød. Fot. Vagn Hansen for Udenrigsministeriet.

KONGEFAMILIEN
HJEMME OG I UDLANDET

Tillæg til Berlingske Tidende Fredag 16. November 1951

as her husband incarnated what people considered to be the qualities of a real man.

A few years after the accession Frederik IX described his aim for his reign with the usual modesty, "I hope that the Queen and I won't go down in history as the very worst in the long lineage."

New Times in the Royal Family

The new Royal Couple managed in general to transform an old, rather rigid Royal Family into a warm and humane one. This was the case not just with the furnishings, which thanks to Queen Ingrid were brought up to date, but also in the modes of address and in ceremonial terms. Frederik IX replaced, for example, the word "banquet" with "party", and saw to it that the annual gatherings for the government and the parliament became more lively, with musical entertainment and a standing buffet.

It can be said that the centre of gravity was moved from the King to the Royal Family when Frederik IX took over. His family became the epitome of the postwar Danish nuclear family, and the Royal Couple appeared to a far higher degree than their predecessors to be a couple with a shared life, in which they collaborated on the challenges posed by everyday tasks. An entirely different openness was established around the Royal Family, as Frederik IX and Queen Ingrid gladly allowed the public to follow the upbringing of their children.

Queen Ingrid did both the family and the country a service a few years after the accession by seeing to it that her husband dried out. Frederik IX had a habit of being "indisposed" at unfortunate moments, and it had gradually become clear to everyone that his use of alcohol had reached a level that was incompatible with his position. That antabuse was launched in 1948 perhaps made the decision easier, but in any case the King stopped drinking overnight and never touched alcohol again. Instead he thereafter drank tomato juice and litres of fizzy drinks, and increased his already high consumption of cigarettes.

Around the same time as Frederik IX's change of lifestyle occurred, he began to live out his musical passion to a higher degree than he had previously

Supplement about the Royal Family in the newspaper Berlingske Tidende from 16 November 1951. Frederik IX and Queen Ingrid allowed the public greater insight into family life than their predecessors, and to the populace they appeared to be the ideal nuclear family.

The Royal Family on a bench in Fredensborg Palace Gardens on 5 June 1953, a new Act of Succession having been signed earlier in the day.

allowed himself. In 1948, he conducted the Royal Orchestra during sessions that resulted in three records which were made the prizes in a charity lottery in connection with UN aid. The King refrained from conducting in public as he found it inappropriate, but many of the musicians he worked with at private concerts uniformly attested that Frederik IX was an excellent conductor with a natural authority and a highly developed musicality. One of the annual highlights for Frederik IX was the concert the Royal Orchestra gave each year as a birthday present, and over the course of time he conducted a broad repertoire which amongst other things included most of Beethoven's symphonies. It was on the other hand the cause of great sorrow for Frederik IX that he lost his most important musical ally when Queen Alexandrine died in 1952. Although she was outwardly very modest, his mother had played a central role in the Royal Family on the home front.

A decisive event in the early phase of the reign was the ratification of the Act of Succession in 1953. The press had begun to air the possibility of a change of law as early as the late 1940s, and it was far from obvious to the populace why male succession should be maintained. The time was not yet ripe for full gender equality in the order of succession (this was first introduced in 2009), so the solution was a conditional order of succession which allowed daughters to inherit the throne if there wasn't a son who had right of succession. The question of the order of succession was coupled with a long wished for revision of the Constitution, because the former could entice people out to vote and therefore make it possible to adopt the latter. The result of the vote meant that Princess Margrethe became the new heir to the throne of Denmark.

The Daughters Fly the Nest

While the 1950s were characterized by family life, the Act of Succession, music, and extensive travel activity, the 1960s brought other challenges to the Royal Family. The princesses became grown women who got married and started families, while Frederik IX truly established himself as the beloved national patriarch as which he is still remembered.

The first of the daughters to be chosen was Princess Anne-Marie. She and the Greek Crown Prince Constantine had fallen in love at his sister's wedding in

The Royal Family taking afternoon tea at Amalienborg. For the busy family their afternoon tea at 4 pm was an anchor in everyday life, during which there was rarely time to gather for meals. Picture from the recordings of the film Danmarks Konge (Denmark's King) which was made between 1955 and 1957.

Five years after being elected as heir to the throne, Princess Margrethe turned 18 and became a member of the Privy Council. The princess sits between her father and the Finance Minister Viggo Kampmann (later Prime Minister).

and King Constantine couldn't take part, as they a few months earlier had in effect been taken hostage in their own country because of the military coup in Greece.

The last to get married was Princess Benedikte, who met the German Prince Richard, 6th Prince of Sayn-Wittgenstein-Berleburg, at a ball in Amsterdam in March 1966. The engagement was declared a year later, but several points of constitutional law relevant to the relationship had to be modified, so that Princess Benedikte could remain in the order of succession and serve as regent. This was a form of precaution for the Royal Family, since Princess Anne-Marie had with her marriage left the order of succession, but it was possible to take the necessary measures so that the wedding could be held on 3 February 1968.

Frederik IX had the opportunity to conduct the Royal Orchestra with the Swiss piano virtuoso Edwin Fischer as soloist on two occasions. Here they are seen during a rehearsal in 1954.

Athens in 1962, but because of her young age they had to keep it secret from their parents for a time before the Crown Prince dared to ask Frederik IX for his daughter's hand in marriage. The request gave rise to an amusing episode in which the King ordered the Greek Crown Prince out into the toilet next to his office while he spoke to Queen Ingrid about the marriage. The Royal Couple agreed to the marriage, but insisted that the wedding be deferred until their daughter was of age. The marriage was held in Athens on 18 September 1964, and in the meantime Constantine had become king, so Princess Anne-Marie became the Queen of Greece at the ceremony.

The engagement of the heir to the throne, Princess Margrethe, came as a surprise to everyone outside the immediate family. The marriage to Count Henri Marie Jean André de Laborde de Monpezat in Holmen Church in Copenhagen on 10 June 1967 was, on the other hand, a grand occasion which two million Danish viewers followed on TV. The only great negative point was that Queen Anne-Marie

The wedding in
Holmen Church on
10 June 1967 be-
tween Crown Prin-
cess Margrethe and
Count Henri, whom
we know today as
the Prince Consort.
The proud parents
are seen closest to
the bride.

The marriages soon led to the expected results in the form of Princess Alex-
ia (1965), Crown Prince Pavlos (1967), Prince Frederik (1968), Prince Joachim
(1969), Prince Gustav (1969), Prince Nikolaos (1969), and Princess Alexandra
(1970). After Frederik IX's death came Princess Nathalie (1975), Princess The-
odora (1983) and Prince Philippos (1986).

Frederik IX's Final Years

After their daughters had left the home the Royal Couple had a quieter life. The
King liked to spend his free time taking long drives in his beloved cars and continued to cultivate his interest in hunting. On account of his lungs, the chain-smok-
ing king was forced to change to smoking a pipe, and in a short space of time he
built up a large collection. Official travel activities of course continued and took

Princess Anne-Ma-
rie's wedding to
King Constantine
in Athens on 18
September 1964.
Besides affection
for each other, the
couple had – and
have – in common
that they are both
descendants of the
first Glücksburg
King and Queen,
Christian IX and
Queen Louise. Their
next-eldest son,
Prince Vilhelm, was
chosen as King of
Greece and called
George I.

Frederik IX, Queen
Ingrid, and their
three daughters,
from the left: Prin-
cess Benedikte,
Princess Anne-Ma-
rie, and the heir to
the throne Princess
Margrethe, now the
reigning Queen of
Denmark. Official
photo from August
1964.
The family portrait
was taken on the
occasion of, and
just prior to, Prin-
cess Anne-Marie's
18th birthday. Mem-
bers of the Danish
Royal Family don't
bear the Order of
the Elephant on the
characteristic light
blue sash until they
come of age, just
as there is a tradi-
tion that princesses
don't wear a dia-
dem until they have
turned eighteen.

Frederik IX holds his first televised New Year Speech in 1959. The New Year Speech stems from the toast the King has for centuries made to the kingdom at the New Year banquet. Frederik VIII augmented this custom with a speech in 1909, which then became a tradition. When Christian X's New Year Speech was transmitted on the radio for the first time in 1941, the speech had a markedly greater impact, but it was Frederik IX's televised speeches which made the New Year Speech the vital connection between the monarch and the populace which it continues to be. In terms of form Her Majesty the Queen's New Year Speeches keep to the format laid down by Frederik IX. The speech has no introductory greeting, but usually begins with a reflection on the turn of the year, followed by an account of the year that has passed, both in Denmark and abroad, as well as within the Royal Family.

the Royal Couple to both Africa and the Middle East, just as Queen Ingrid continued to see to a great burden of work with her many official duties.

Frederik IX's last major feast day was his 70th birthday on 11 March 1969. For the occasion he made an appearance in a TV interview, where, with a pipe in his mouth, he spoke about his life and appeared considerably aged, but also at peace. At the end of the interview the King remarked, accurately enough, that "One is first and foremost one's self".

Towards the end of 1971 Frederik IX's health began to worsen, and thereafter his memory began to fail him too. In spite of his background as a sportsman, he had pushed himself overly hard throughout his life, both with regard to work and unhealthy habits. In his final years he lost some of his characteristic presence and good humour, but it can also be said that his aim in life had by that time been fulfilled. He had redefined the Royal Family so that it could adopt an up-to-date place in the welfare state, won the hearts of

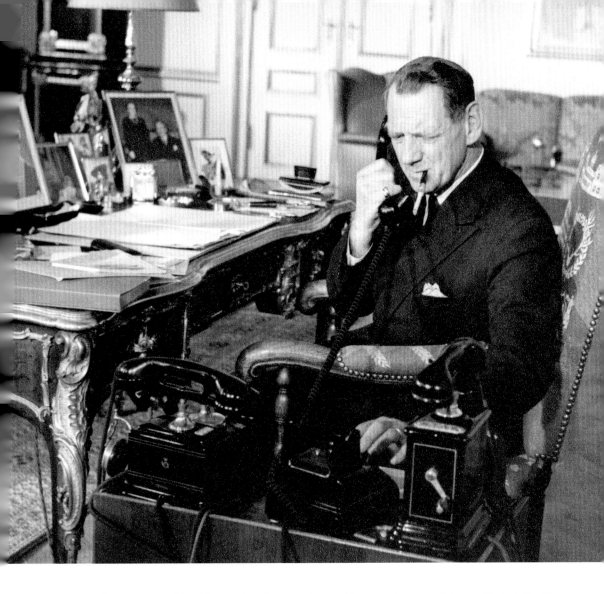

Danes, secured the future order of succession, and in general seen and done more than anyone could realistically hope for.

On New Year's Eve the King fell ill and had to be admitted to Kommunehospitalet (the municipal hospital), and although for a few days it looked as though he would recover, his condition worsened as his lung infection presumably re-

Frederik IX at his desk in Fredensborg Palace.

Dybbøl Mill seen shot to pieces after the battles of 1864, during which Denmark suffered a humiliating defeat. On the 100th anniversary of the Battle of Dybbøl Frederik IX held an impromptu speech which was the most controversial of his reign. He said, amongst other things, of the Danish soldiers, "They knew only one thing: Hold out, carry on! They fell in the end, but they fell in honour of our old land". The King was speaking as a patriotic officer and as the great-grandchild of Christian IX, who had to begin his reign by signing the fatal November Constitution, which caused the war. Nonetheless the speech met with criticism from several quarters, since many thought that he had defied the Danish tradition of neutrality that had developed after 1864.

sulted in a stroke. On 14 January 1972 at 7.50 pm Frederik IX died surrounded by his family, and the following day Prime Minister Jens Otto Krag proclaimed Queen Margrethe II the new head of state from the balcony of Christiansborg Palace.

Queen Ingrid after Frederik IX

The death of the King was naturally a great loss and changed Queen Ingrid's life drastically. She had, however, plenty of experience from her childhood in tackling loss and solitude, and again she demonstrated the same resilience which had got her through her teenage years. Like Queen Alexandrine she

In 1970 Frederik IX and Queen Ingrid went on one of their last big journeys together, which took them to Tanzania, Ethiopia, and Kenya. The Royal Couple visited the Ethiopian Emperor Haile Selassie, who was deposed four years later in a military coup. Rastafarians worship Selassie as the Second Coming.

The German President Gustav Heinemann on an official visit in 1971. It can be sensed that Frederik IX wasn't entirely positive about Denmark's neighbours to the south.

Queen Ingrid with her grandchildren in Gråsten Palace Gardens in 1975. The palace gardens were one of Queen Ingrid's great passions, and after Frederik IX's death she had time to seriously devote herself to gardening at the Fredensborg and Gråsten Palaces in particular.

did not wish to be styled "Queen Dowager", but retained the title of Queen in concordance with the wishes of her eldest daughter. Queen Ingrid created a meaningful life for herself in Kancellihuset (the Chancellery) at Fredensborg Palace, where she concentrated on the well-being of the palace gardens and the children. At the same time she continued her work as chairman and patron of a number of organizations and institutions and was able as the first and so far only person outside the order of succession to act as regent while the Monarch was abroad.

As the focal point of the family Queen Ingrid ensured that unity was maintained, amongst other things by arranging regular family gatherings at Gråsten Palace which were reminiscent of the mythologized Fredensborg Days of Christian IX and Queen Louise's time. Of course, Queen Ingrid had most importance for the two grandchildren who lived closest by, Crown Prince Frederik and Prince Joachim, who had busy parents and often visited their grandmother. Queen Ingrid became a solid mentor for the Crown Prince in particular, and played her part in preparing him for his life of responsibilities in the public eye.

Queen Ingrid in June 1998 in the company of Crown Prince Frederik. The occasion is the marriage of her grandchild Princess Alexandra of Berleburg to Count Jefferson von Pfeil und Klein-Ellguth. Due to osteoporosis Queen Ingrid used a walking frame in her final years. This meant that many older Danes with difficulty walking began to use this aid. Because of the Queen's example the municipal aid centres registered a significant rise in the demand for walking frames.

As the 1990s wore on, Queen Ingrid's formerly so elegant and erect person slumped more and more, though her spirit was undimmed. It became more and more obvious that she didn't have long to live, but on Queen Margrethe II's Silver Jubilee on 14 January 1997 she held, to everyone's surprise, a moving speech for her daughter, which she rounded off with the following words, "And Daisy, you have two wonderful sons, so I think I can safely shut my eyes, and they will do their best for Denmark." Queen Ingrid's quiet death in the afternoon of 7 November 2000 was the cause of justified national grief.

Frederik IX and Queen Ingrid are the only Royal Couple to be buried outdoors outside Roskilde Cathedral. In Christian iconography the anchor is a symbol of hope, but here it simultaneously bears witness to an actual sailor's life.

Crown Prince
Frederik and
Princess Ingrid
at their engagement
in March 1935.

The Reign in Retrospect

It is difficult, indeed very difficult, to find any negative opinions about Frederik IX and Queen Ingrid. This can partly be explained by the time in which they reigned, for after the occupation the Royal Family rode on a wave of popularity. But the absence of criticism is first and foremost due to the fact that Frederik IX and Queen Ingrid served in their roles with warmth, intelligence, and a never failing certainty of style.

Frederik IX appeared to a much higher degree than his predecessors to be a man of the people, but at the same time remained in a class of his own. It was peculiar to him that he could have such a broad appeal, that all layers of society could see themselves reflected in him. The swearing, tattooed sailor ought really to have stood in contrast to the highly educated and well-read music expert, who Frederik IX also was, but his personality housed these quite different elements without people finding it false. The breadth of the King's activities was possible quite simply because he was good at his job. Both ship's crews, members of court, and orchestra musicians could tell of a boss who cheerfully and perspicaciously knew how to get everyone to give their best.

It is, however, worth reflecting on whether Frederik IX's reputation would have been just as positive if he had grown ten years older, for there is no doubt that much of what happened in the 1970s would have been foreign to him. His view of the world had its roots in the 1800s, and he looked on in wonder at the new tendencies of the 1960s – long hair and pop music, for example, were completely incomprehensible to him.

If a single person were to be highlighted with regard to the Royal Family's continued massive popular support, it would have to be Queen Ingrid. Thanks to her influence Frederik IX endowed his reign with a dignity he probably wouldn't have found by himself. As Royal Couple they together mastered the art of being both popular and regal in a time in which the handling of the media became ever more defining for the monarchy. With their "informal formality" Frederik IX and Queen Ingrid managed to balance between the inclusive and the exalted in a way which has been an example to the new generations of the Royal Family in Denmark.

SUGGESTIONS FOR FURTHER READING

In Danish unless otherwise stated.

Bistrup, Annelise: *Dronning Ingrid.* Aschehoug 1997
– Biography of Queen Ingrid. Describes the Queen's life and work up until the time of publication a few years before her death.

Buchwaldt, Randi/Rosvall, Ted: *Ingrid 1910-2000.*
Falköbing Rosvall Royal Books 2010
– Richly illustrated analysis of the Queen's life.

Lerche, Anna/Marcus Mandal: *A Royal Family.*
Aschehoug, 2003 (in English, also available as a TV series on DVD)
– Richly illustrated book about Christian IX, Queen Louise, and their descendants.

Møller, Jes Fabricius: *Dynastiet Glücksborg – En danmarkshistorie.*
Gads Forlag, 2013
– Recent publication about the House of Glücksburg with in-depth analyses of the monarchy's role and development in Denmark.

Røllum-Larsen, Claus: *Kong Frederik IX og musikken – Musikhistoriske studier i det danske Kongehus.* Poul Kristensens Forlag, 1990
– An exhaustive survey of Frederik IX's musical activities.

Skipper, Jon Bloch: *Sømandskongen – En biografi om Frederik IX.*
Aschehoug, 2005
– The latest biography of Frederik IX; it is thorough, entertaining, and richly illustrated. The book is also to a large degree about Queen Ingrid.

Skipper, Jon Bloch: *Tre søstre – samtaler mellem*
Dronning Margrethe, Prinsesse Benedikte og Dronning Anne-Marie.
Lindhardt og Ringhof 2008.
– Amongst other topics, the three sisters discuss their parents.

Frederik IX and Queen Ingrid
The Modern Royal Couple

Copyright © 2015
The Royal Danish Collection and Historika / Gads Forlag A/S

ISBN: 978-87-93229-08-2
Second edition, first print run

Printed in Lithuania

Text: Jens Gunni Busck
Edited by Birgit Jenvold
Translated from Danish by Christopher Sand-Iversen
Cover and graphic design Lene Nørgaard, Propel
Printed by Clemenstrykkeriet, Lithuania

Illustrations:
P. 34-35 Polfoto, p. 45-46 Rigmor Mydtskov, p. 53, 54 Scanpix, p. 55 Hanne Posche. All other illustrations: Kongernes Samling

Photocopying may only be undertaken at institutions that have concluded agreements with COPY-Dan and may only be undertaken within the limitations established by the agreement in question.

CO_2 neutrale tryksager
KLIMANEUTRALISERET
Cert.nr. 0017/DK

MIX
Paper from responsible sources
FSC® C122712
www.fsc.org